Jedediah Smith

Jedediah Smith

Sharlene and Ted Nelson

Franklin Watts
A Division of Scholastic Inc.
New York • Toronto • London • Auckland • Sydney
Mexico City • New Delhi • Hong Kong
Danbury, Connecticut

Dedicated to the historians whose publications made this book possible as well as the Jedediah Smith Society and its members, especially James C. Auld, Dr. Haworth Clover, James Hardee, Wayne Knauf, and Joseph Molter.

Note to readers: Definitions for words in **bold** can be found in the Glossary at the back of this book.

Photographs ©2004: Bancroft Library, University of California, Berkeley: 31 (Mission San Gabriel, by Vischer, The Mission Era: California Under Spain and Mexico and Reminiscences, 19xx.03909-ALB); Bridgeman Art Library International Ltd., London/New York: 30 (Private Collection); Clymer Museum of Art: 21 (Survival, by John F. Clymer, reproduced with permission of Mrs. John F. Clymer); Corbis Images: 35 (David Ball), 42 (Kevin R. Morris), 34 (Royalty-Free), 36 (Ron Watts); Greater St. Charles Convention Bureau: 12 (Brett Dufer/Pebble Publishing, replica keelboat built by Discovery Exedition, Saint Charles, MO); Jeff Vanuga: 2, 16, 46; Joslyn Art Museum, Omaha, Nebraska: 14 (Malcolm Varon), 17, 24 (Malcolm Varon/Gift of Enron Art Foundation); Minden Pictures/Tim Fitzharris: 20; Missouri Historical Society, St. Louis, MO: 10 (by George Catlin), 8; North Wind Picture Archives: 5 right, 11, 32, 39, 50; Photo Researchers, NY/Thomas and Pat Leeson: 9; Scotts Bluff National Monument, Gering, NE/William Henry Jackson Collection: 5 left, 26, 27, 48; South Dakota Art Museum: 18 (Jedediah Smith in the Badlands, Harvey Dunn, 1947); Walters Art Museum, Baltimore: 29, 45; Washington State Historical Society, Tacoma: 41 (from Picturesque California, Sec. 6, pg. 249), 44 (Port McL 4), 23 (Port/ODG 1); Washington State University Libraries: 6 (MASC, George Mathis Collection, Box 2, Folder 59).

Cover illustration by Stephen Marchesi.
Map by XNR Productions, Inc.

The illustration on the cover shows the U.S. explorer Jedediah Smith. The photograph opposite the title page shows the Rocky Mountains.

Library of Congress Cataloging-in-Publication Data

Nelson, Sharlene P.
    Jedediah Smith / by Sharlene and Ted Nelson.
        p. cm. — (Watts library)
    Summary: Discusses the life and work of Jedediah Smith, an explorer of the American West and leader of the mountain men.
Includes bibliographical references (p.) and index.
    ISBN 0-531-12287-5 (lib. bdg.)   0-531-16676-7 (pbk.)
    1. Smith, Jedediah Strong, 1799-1831—Juvenile literature. 2. Pioneers—West (U.S.)—Biography—Juvenile literature. 3. Explorers—West (U.S.)—Biography—Juvenile literature. 4. Trappers—West (U.S.)—Biography—Juvenile literature. 5. Frontier and pioneer life—West (U.S.)—Juvenile literature. 6. West (U.S.)—History—To 1848—Juvenile literature. 8. West (U.S.)—Biography—Juvenile literature. [1. Smith, Jedediah Strong, 1799-1831. 2. Explorers. 3. West (U.S.)—Discovery and exploration.] I. Nelson, Ted W. II. Title. III. Series.
F592.S649N45 2003
978'.02'092—dc22

       2003013344

Contents

Jedediah Smith lived before photography. An artist painted this portrait based on later photographs of Smith family members.

Chapter One

A Young Man of Enterprise

In February of 1822, Jedediah Strong Smith was in St. Louis, Missouri, looking for work. He read an advertisement in the *Missouri Gazette & Public Advertiser* with great interest. The ad was addressed "To Enterprising Young Men." It stated, "The subscriber wishes to engage ONE HUNDRED MEN to ascend the river Missouri to its sources, there to be employed for one, two or three years." Anyone interested was to contact General William H. Ashley.

TO Enterprising Young Men.

THE subscriber wishes to engage ONE HUN-DRED MEN, to ascend the river Missouri to its source, there to be employed for one, two or three years.—For particulars, enquire of Major Andrew Henry, near the Lead Mines, in the County of Washington, (who will ascend with, and command the party) or to the subscriber at St. Louis.

Wm. H. Ashley.

Smith's adventurous career began when he answered this February 1822 advertisement in a St. Louis newspaper.

Smith hurried through the streets of St. Louis and presented himself to General Ashley. Smith was twenty-three years old. He was 6 feet (183 centimeters) tall and had brown hair and blue eyes. Smith made an immediate impression on the general, who later described him as very intelligent and worthy of trust.

General Ashley explained that he and Major Andrew Henry were looking for men to work in the beaver fur trade. General Ashley was a prominent Missouri politician and businessman. Major Henry had previously led fur trappers to the Rocky Mountains. Both had served in the Missouri **militia** before becoming business partners.

Smith was employed as a hunter by General Ashley. Smith wrote in his journal that he "found no difficulty in making a bargain on as good terms as I had reason to expect." Thus, one of the most adventurous careers in the history of the American West was about to begin.

Young Jedediah

Jedediah Smith was born on January 6, 1799, in Jericho, New York. The little town on the banks of the Susquehanna River is now called Bainbridge. He was the fourth child born to Jedediah Smith Sr. and his wife Sally. Sally's maiden name, Strong, was given to Jedediah as his middle name.

The Smiths had eight more children, but three girls died when they were young, leaving Jedediah with two sisters and six brothers.

When Jedediah was twelve years old, his family moved to Pennsylvania on the shores of Lake Erie. There, the Smiths became good friends with the family of Dr. Titus Gordon Vespasian Simons. Doctor Simons became a **mentor** to young Jedediah and taught him spelling and penmanship.

Smith family lore says Jedediah became interested in the West when the doctor gave him a copy of the *Journals of Lewis and Clark*. The two explorers, Captains Meriwether Lewis and William Clark, were sent west by President Thomas Jefferson. They left from near St. Louis in 1804 and reached the Pacific Ocean at the mouth of the Columbia River in 1805. They returned a year later. They were the first U.S. citizens to cross the North American continent.

When Jedediah was eighteen, the Smith and Simons families moved to Ohio in search of new land and new opportunities. The families built small farms,

Beaver and the Fur Trade

Beaver are mammals belonging to the rodent family. They can weigh more than 60 pounds (27 kilograms). Using their sharp teeth, they chew down small trees and use them to build homes of sticks and mud in rivers and streams. Europeans began trapping beaver in eastern North America in the 1600s. The beaver's short inner fur was used to make hats. In the early 1800s, mountain men began trapping beaver in the West. Fur trading companies took the furs east, where they were sold for high prices.

St. Louis became an important U.S. city after the Louisiana Purchase of 1803.

and Jedediah Sr. worked for meager wages as a tailor. To help feed and support his family, Jedediah became an expert hunter. In 1821, he left home and headed to St. Louis at the edge of the western frontier.

The Frontier's Edge

When Jedediah Smith arrived in St. Louis, he found a bustling city. It was on the west bank of the Mississippi River, near its **confluence** with the Missouri River. This once tiny French town had become an important U.S. city since the Louisiana Purchase was completed.

A colorful collection of people crowded the city's streets. American Indians from the **Great Plains** pitched their **tepees** on vacant lots and waited to see William Clark. The famous explorer had become the United States superintendent of

The Louisiana Purchase

President Thomas Jefferson acquired lands from France in 1803. The purchase extended the United States's boundary westward from the Mississippi River to the Rocky Mountains.

10

Indian affairs in the West. Trail-worn men rode their horses past taverns and shops. They had been to the Mexican settlement of Santa Fe. At that time, Mexico's lands extended from the eastern Gulf of Mexico to the Mexican province of California.

Fur trappers, who had traveled to the Rocky Mountains along the route followed by Lewis and Clark, wore **buckskins** stained with buffalo grease. They told Smith about fierce bears and the many Indian tribes in the West. They talked about Britain's Hudson's Bay Company trappers searching for beaver beyond the Rocky Mountains, where the Snake and Columbia Rivers flowed.

In his mind, Smith imagined a map of the West. Beyond the Rocky Mountains, there was a vast region known only to the Indians who had lived there for thousands of years. Smith later wrote, "I wa[nted] to be the first to view a country on which the eyes of a white man had never gazed and to follow the course of rivers that run through a new land."

Fur trappers, who had been up the Missouri River, roamed the streets of St. Louis.

11

Smith headed up the Missouri River aboard a keelboat similar to the one shown in this photograph.

Chapter Two

The Adventures Begin

In early May of 1822, Smith headed up the Missouri River toward the Yellowstone River aboard a **keelboat**. It was 1,600 miles (2,575 kilometers) away. The boat was loaded with supplies and crowded with trappers, hunters, and boaters. A square sail hung from a mast, but the boaters usually rowed or **poled** the boat against the river's swift current. Sometimes, they walked on shore and pulled the heavy craft with ropes attached to the mast.

Only 200 miles (320 km) up the Missouri River, the mast of the cumbersome boat struck an overhanging tree. The boat spun and then sank. Nearly $10,000 worth of supplies were lost. While Smith and the men camped on shore, one man returned to St. Louis to tell General Ashley of the loss.

On to the Yellowstone River

General Ashley arrived in late June with another keelboat and picked up the stranded men. As the boat crept slowly up the river, Smith walked along the shore, hunting for **game**. Smith wrote of finding "Black bear, Deer, Elk, Raccoon [sic], and Turkeys in abundance. And as the Country was well stocked with Bees[,] we frequently had a plentiful supply of honey."

Smith hunted along the shore while the keelboat made its slow progress up the Missouri River.

In September, the keelboat reached the villages of the Arikara Indians. The Yellowstone River was still 400 miles (640 km) away. Worried about the keelboat's slow pace, Ashley acquired horses from the Arikara. With a few men, including Smith, he rode toward the Yellowstone River.

Ashley's overland party reached the Yellowstone River in early October. Henry and his men greeted them. Their keelboat had left St. Louis in April. They had built a rough log fort near the Yellowstone. After Ashley's keelboat arrived, he headed back to St. Louis to gather supplies for next year.

While Smith hunted for game, the trappers hunted for beaver. The trappers preferred to hunt beaver in the late fall and early spring. Furs taken then were the most valuable.

Winter on the Musselshell

In November, Smith joined a group of Henry's men on the Musselshell River. Some men began preparing their winter camp by building crude log houses. "I took some of the best hunters and made every exertion to procure a supply of meat sufficient for our suport [sic]," wrote Smith. "Our houses being finished we were well prepared for the increasing cold." The cold came, and the river froze. Smith described ice so thick that he watched buffalo "in vast Bands that came from the north and crossed over [the river] to the south side on the ice."

In the spring of 1823, Smith returned to the fort where he found a worried Henry. His trappers needed more horses to reach remote rivers and streams. Henry entrusted Smith with a

The Trappers' Trade

A trapper would set iron traps, each weighing about 6 pounds (2.7 kg), in shallow water. A chain on the trap attached to a pole set in deeper water kept the beaver from carrying the trap away. Above the trap, the trapper placed a stick smeared with **castoreum**, a strong-smelling substance from a beaver's **castor glands**. Attracted by the scent, a beaver would step on the trap and drown. The trapper would skin the beaver, save the castoreum, and dry the skin with its fur on a hoop of sticks. After collecting one hundred furs, the trapper would pack them tightly in deerskin bags for shipment.

Buffalo, such as these, crossed the frozen river in vast herds near the trappers' winter camp.

message for Ashley asking him to buy horses from the Arikara. Weeks later, Smith met Ashley coming up the Missouri River with two keelboats carrying supplies and ninety men.

A Surprise Attack

At the Arikara villages, Ashley went ashore with caution. Recently, two warriors had been killed in a battle with another fur trading company. Still, they sold Ashley several horses. Smith and forty men remained on shore to guard the animals.

Ashley was hoping to buy more horses when the Arikara attacked. They fired on the boats and charged the men on shore. Smith and some of the men fired their rifles at the warriors to protect other members of the party who were leaping into the river. Finally, Smith jumped to safety. One man later wrote, "When his party was in danger, Mr. Smith was always among the foremost to meet it, and the last to fly; those who

16

saw him on shore at the [Arikara] fight, in 1823, can attest to the truth of this assertion."

Ashley retreated downriver. Fifteen men had been killed and nine wounded. Others wanted to return to St. Louis. Ashley sent them back in one keelboat. He instructed them to leave the supplies at Fort Kiowa in present-day South Dakota. Those who remained camped on an island and buried their lost comrades. At the burial, Smith expressed his Christian beliefs. He "made a powerful prayer, which moved us all greatly," wrote one trapper.

Ashley needed more men. Smith volunteered to return to the Yellowstone River with a message asking Henry for help. With one companion, he set out on foot. A month later, Smith, Henry, and fifty men arrived at Ashley's camp. By then, the United States Army had been alerted to the threat posed by the Arikara. Ashley's men joined the soldiers and attacked the Arikara. A peace treaty was signed, and the Arikara left their villages. Ashley, Henry, and their men traveled downriver to Fort Kiowa.

Proud Arikara Indians fought to protect their homeland from the trappers.

Trappers and Tribes

In their search for beaver, the trappers encountered many different Indian tribes. The tribes often guided the trappers and gave them food and horses in exchange for beads, blankets, and guns. But conflicts occurred. Many tribes fought to protect their homeland and way of life or to avenge trappers' wrongs against tribal members.

Smith led a small brigade westward from Fort Kiowa in 1823.

Chapter Three

Across the Continental Divide

At Fort Kiowa, the men gathered their supplies. Ashley and Henry had to resume trapping or their business would be ruined. But returning west by keelboat was too slow and dangerous. In the future, their men would travel in **brigades**. They would travel overland on horseback with horses and mules carrying their supplies.

The Trappers' Brigades

Large brigades included a leader, trappers, hunters, a clerk to keep records, and men to tend the animals and perform camp chores.

After obtaining horses, Henry led a brigade back to the Yellowstone River. Ashley selected Smith to lead a small brigade to search farther west for beaver. With him were James Clyman, Thomas Fitzpatrick, and William Sublette. They set out in late September with their supply-laden horses.

Attacked by a Grizzly

Near the Black Hills in present-day South Dakota, the men walked through a thicket. Suddenly, a grizzly bear leaped onto Smith. It grabbed Smith's head in its jaws and threw him to the

Fierce grizzly bears were a menace to all trappers.

ground, tearing his scalp and one ear loose. One man killed the bear while Clyman rushed to aid Smith.

According to Clyman, Smith said, "if you have a needle and thread[,] git [get] it out and sew up my wound around my head." Clyman sewed the scalp back on, but said he "could do nothing for his Eare [ear]." Smith replied, "O you must try to stitch [it] up one way or other." Clyman carefully positioned the **lacerated** parts together. "Then I put in my needle[,] stiching [sic] it through and through and over and over," until he had sewn Smith's ear in place. When Smith could travel,

On a cold winter day in March 1824, Smith and his men feasted on raw buffalo meat at South Pass.

21

they pushed west and spent the winter with Crow Indians on the Wind River in present-day Wyoming.

Across the Divide

In February of 1824, they set out again. Winds blew heavy snow. At night, the men lay awake, hanging on to their blankets. They found little game. It was often impossible to start fires. Tiny sparks produced by striking flint and steel together blew away in the wind. Late in March, they reached a broad, rolling plain. With shouts of joy, Clyman and Sublette shot a buffalo. The men had not eaten for days, and they eagerly ate the meat raw.

In the excitement of the buffalo kill, Smith scarcely noticed that they had reached South Pass on the **Continental Divide**. To their backs, the rivers flowed toward the Atlantic Ocean. Ahead, the rivers flowed toward the Pacific Ocean. Other U.S. trappers had crossed the pass going east in 1812, as they were returning from the Columbia River. But Smith and his men were the first to cross the pass going west.

Beyond the divide, Smith and his men trapped along the Green River in present-day southwest Wyoming and northeast Utah. Beaver were plentiful. In June, they took their furs back across South Pass and opened a cache they had made in the spring. Then they covered a framework of saplings with buffalo hide to make a **bullboat**. Fitzpatrick and two men would use the boat to carry the furs downriver to St. Louis. Despite their successful trapping, the men were sad. Clyman had

The Trappers' Cache

A hole was dug in the ground and filled with supplies and furs for temporary storage. The cache was covered with dirt to hide it.

disappeared. They feared that hostile Indians had killed him.

Into Oregon Country

Smith, Sublette, and five other men said goodbye to Fitzpatrick and headed north into Oregon country. Britain and the United States had agreed that this vast area west of the Rocky Mountains and north of lands claimed by Mexico was open to the citizens of both nations. However, the trappers of Britain's Hudson's Bay Company wanted to keep this rich beaver country for themselves. When Smith and his men reached a Hudson's Bay Company post in present-day western Montana, they were considered more as "spies than trappers." Still, they were treated kindly.

Peter Skene Ogden led Hudson's Bay Company trappers.

In December, Smith and his men joined a Hudson's Bay Company brigade led by Peter Skene Ogden. As they traveled south through heavy snows, a rivalry grew between the Hudson's Bay men and the Americans. Each group wanted to show that its members were better trappers. Smith's men trapped more beaver than Ogden's men did and proved they were the best. Smith exchanged many of the furs with Ogden for supplies. In April, Smith and his men left Ogden to look for Ashley.

The First Rendezvous

In July of 1825, Smith found Ashley and his men gathered near the Green River. This was the trappers' first **rendezvous**. These summertime meetings, held at a prearranged place, occurred annually from 1825 to 1840. Many old friends greeted Smith, including Thomas Fitzpatrick and James Clyman. After being separated from Smith, Clyman had wandered on foot for eighty days before reaching a U.S. fort.

Ashley came with supplies from St. Louis. The trappers came with furs. They exchanged their furs for gunpowder, ammunition, sugar, coffee, and tobacco as well as blankets and beads for trading with the Indians. With fresh supplies,

After the rendezvous of 1825, Smith and Ashley carried their rich cargo of furs down the Missouri River on a government keelboat.

the men of the brigades could survive another year in the mountains.

Henry had decided to retire, and Ashley selected Smith to be his new partner. Ashley and Smith headed back to St. Louis with nearly 9,000 pounds (4,082 kg) of furs. When they reached St. Louis in October, the *Missouri Advocate* newspaper reported that they came with "one of the richest cargoes of fur that ever arrived in St. Louis."

A month later, Smith started west with men, horses, and supplies. Snow trapped them on the Great Plains, and two men walked back to St. Louis to inform Ashley. In the spring, Ashley arrived with more horses and supplies. Then they all traveled to the rendezvous in Cache Valley in present-day Utah, near the Great Salt Lake.

The Great Salt Lake

This is a large lake that has no outlets. Freshwater entering the lake is lost to **evaporation**, leaving salt behind. The lake is several times saltier than the ocean.

At the rendezvous,
trappers and Indians
gathered for trade
and fun.

Chapter Four

On to California

The rendezvous of 1826 was a festive affair. Trappers who had married Indian women came with their families. Tepees made by several Indian tribes stood among the trappers' tents. The men of the brigades joined with the Indians in "Mirth, songs, dancing, shouting, trading, running, jumping, singing, races, [and] target-shooting," wrote one trapper.

In exchange for supplies, Ashley received enough furs to make him rich. He sold his interest in the fur trade to his most trusted men: Jedediah Smith, David Jackson, and William Sublette. The new company was named Smith, Jackson & Sublette.

Into the Unknown

The ambitious young partners wanted to expand their business. As Smith wrote in his journal, he thought that the rivers and streams to the west might be "well stocked with beaver." The partners also wanted to find a river called the Buenaventura. **Mountain men** believed that the Buenaventura flowed from the Rocky Mountains through California and on to the Pacific Ocean. While Jackson's and Sublette's brigades trapped beaver in the northern Rocky Mountains, Smith would search for beaver and for the Buenaventura River in the lands to the west.

Smith left his partners in August, promising to return for the next rendezvous. With him were eighteen men, including Harrison Rogers, his clerk and second in command, and fifty horses and mules. Expecting to travel through country with little game, the men stopped to hunt. Several days later, they loaded three horses with 700 pounds (318 kg) of dried buffalo meat.

As they traveled south through present-day Utah, the country became dryer. One day, in hopes of finding water, Smith climbed a hill. "To my great Surprise[,] instead of a River[,] an immense sand plain was before me where the utmost view of my **Glass** could not embrace any appearance

California

The present-day state of California got its name when the Spanish began exploring North America in the early 1500s. The first Spanish settlement was established at San Diego in 1769. California became a part of Mexico in 1821 and a U.S. state in 1850.

of water." Farther south, they found rivers and streams that relieved their thirst, but yielded no beaver.

By early October, they had traveled nearly 700 miles (1,130 km) into a country that Smith described as "Barren Stony hills." More than half the horses had died. The dried buffalo meat was gone. At a village of Mojave Indians on the Colorado River in present-day southern Nevada, they were treated with kindness. "Melons and roasted pumpkins were presented in great abundance," wrote Smith. While there, Smith learned that Mexican settlements in California were ten days' travel to the west.

Trappers prepared for long journeys by hunting buffalo and drying the meat.

Smith's 1826 trek across the southwestern desert was filled with hardship.

Trappers in Mission Country

Smith decided to go to California to obtain horses and supplies. From there, he could travel north to "find beaver and in all probability some considerable river [the Buenaventura]." But he was worried. He feared Mexican officials might consider him a spy and "detain me in prison to the ruin of my business."

The weary men crossed the Mojave Desert and entered California's San Bernardino Valley, where streams flowed and cattle and horses grazed. It "seemed certainly a land of enchantment," wrote Smith. Indians working in fields stared as the men passed. They were seeing the first U.S. citizens to reach California by an overland route.

A little farther west, the men were welcomed at Mission San Gabriel by Father José Sánchez. Father Sánchez was in charge of the **mission** and all those working and living there. It was the most prosperous of the California missions. Two thousand Indians tended vineyards, orchards, gardens, and fields of wheat. They also cared for sheep and hogs and worked in a soap factory, **distillery**, and carpentry shops.

Smith and Rogers were invited to eat with Father Sánchez and the other missionaries. "It was a long time since I had had the pleasure of sitting at a table," wrote Smith, "and never in such company." However, the two felt uncomfortable in their dirty, ragged buckskins.

Leaving his men to enjoy Father Sánchez's hospitality, Smith rode to San Diego to meet with California's governor, José Echeandía. He needed the governor's permission to obtain horses and supplies. As expected, his meetings with the governor were unsatisfactory. "I was looked upon with suspicion," he wrote. Like the Hudson's Bay Company's men, the governor thought he was a spy and not a trapper.

Mission San Gabriel was the most prosperous of the twenty-one California missions.

Sierra Nevada

Sierra Nevada is a mountain range that extends for more than 400 miles (640 km) along the east side of California's Central Valley.

Finally U.S. sea captains whose ships were anchored in San Diego Bay helped Smith. They were engaged in trade with the Mexicans. They convinced the governor that Smith was telling the truth. The governor granted him permission to obtain horses and supplies, but ordered him to go back the way he came.

Disobeying the Governor's Orders

Smith traveled aboard a ship from San Diego to a harbor near Mission San Gabriel. Then, in January of 1827, Smith and his men left the mission. With Father Sánchez's help, they obtained sixty horses and food from the mission's farms.

Smith started back the way he had come. Then, despite the governor's order, he turned north into California's Central Valley. The rivers flowing into the valley from the snow-

A scene such as this greeted Smith and his men traveling toward California's Central Valley at the base of the Sierra Nevada mountain range.

capped Sierra Nevadas were rich in beaver. By the time the men had traveled 300 miles (480 km) up the valley, they had collected 1,500 pounds (680 kg) of furs.

In April, Smith began "marching Eastward toward the Rendezvous in the [Rocky] Mountains which I then looked on as a home." Along a mountain ridge above the present-day American River, the men and horses struggled in deep snow. Seeing nothing but "freezing desolation" ahead, Smith led his men back to the valley, where they camped near the present-day Stanislaus River.

Smith decided to try crossing the mountains again, but this time with fewer men. In late May, he selected Silas Gobel and Robert Evans to go with him. They loaded seven horses and two mules with hay and dried meat. Leaving Rogers and the other men with the furs, Smith promised to return in the fall.

Through Snow and Sand

Only a few days' travel into the mountains, a violent snowstorm struck. Two horses and one mule froze to death. In deep snow, the men and animals struggled over an 8,000-foot- (2,440-meter-) high summit and headed down the mountain's east side. Smith and his two men had become the first white men to cross the Sierra Nevadas. The Great Basin lay ahead.

As they traveled east across the vast basin, Smith wrote that the horses became so weak "we were general[ly] obliged to walk." Smith often went ahead of the men in search of water. When he found none, he returned to Evans and Gobel with

The Great Basin

The Great Basin is a desertlike land that includes most of present-day Nevada and parts of Utah, California, Oregon, and Wyoming.

After taking eight days to cross the Sierra Nevada, Smith and two other men reached the Great Basin.

stories to "discourage them as little as possible." They had "hardly the possibility of killing anything" and ate only a handful of dried meat each day. As the horses died, their meat was dried for food.

After walking nearly 300 miles (480 km), Evans lay down in the hot sand. He could go no farther. Smith and Gobel left him in the shade of a small tree and trudged on. Several miles ahead, "To our expressible joy we found water," wrote Smith. Gobel leaped in. Smith dunked his head and gulped the water. He then carried a kettle full to Evans who drank the entire contents—almost 5 quarts (4.7 liters).

Two days later, Smith saw an expanse of water stretching to the north. "The [Great] Salt Lake a joyful sight was spread before us," he wrote. They were almost to the rendezvous

location. Smith, Gobel, and Evans had become the first U.S. citizens to cross the Great Basin. When they arrived at the rendezvous on July 3, 1827, they had only one horse and one mule. "My return caused a considerable bustle in camp," wrote Smith, "for myself and [my] party had been given up as lost." Jackson and Sublette fired a cannon to celebrate.

The Great Salt Lake was "a joyful sight," wrote Smith.

During Smith's 1827 return to California, he crossed through "Barren Stony hills" as he had the year before.

Chapter Five

A Perilous Journey

At the rendezvous, Jedediah Smith found that Jackson's and Sublette's brigades had enjoyed a successful year of trapping. During the winter, Sublette had gone to St. Louis and returned with fresh supplies. But Smith's furs and men were still in California, and he had not found the Buenaventura River. Ten days after arriving at the rendezvous, Smith headed back to California with eighteen men, some horses, and supplies to last two years.

Tragedy on the Colorado

Traveling south through familiar country, Smith led his men to the Mojave village on the Colorado River. Again, the villagers seemed friendly. However, as Smith later learned and wrote, Governor Echeandía "had instructed the Muchaba [Mojave] Indians not to let any more Americans pass through the country."

After a few days of rest, the brigade began crossing the river. Smith and seven men were almost to the west bank when the Mojave attacked. They killed the ten men on the east bank, including Silas Gobel, and captured the horses and supplies. As four hundred Mojave started toward Smith and his men, he directed two marksmen to open fire. The Mojave retreated, and Smith and the men escaped.

Traveling on foot, often at night to avoid the desert heat, Smith and his men reached the farms of Mission San Gabriel. They obtained food and horses and continued north. In late September, they arrived at Rogers's camp.

An Unwelcome Return

Smith never dreaded the dangers he encountered on the trail, but he did dread seeing Governor Echeandía again. A year earlier, Smith had disobeyed Echeandía's order to leave California the way he had come. However, he needed the governor's permission to secure horses and supplies. Smith traveled to Mission San José and then to the coastal town of Monterey to meet with the governor.

As expected, Echeandía was upset. He considered sending Smith to Mexico City, Mexico, where higher authorities could decide his fate. However, ship captains helped out again, and the governor agreed to let Smith continue on.

Smith sailed north to San Francisco with one of the captains, where he rejoined his men. They sold their furs and bought supplies and extra horses and mules. The animals would bring high prices at the next rendezvous. On a rainy day

In San Francisco, Smith bought horses and mules before leading his men back to California's Central Valley.

San Francisco

In the early 1800s, San Francisco was a small Mexican settlement on San Francisco Bay with a fort, a mission, and a few buildings. Large ranches edged the bay.

in December of 1827, twenty men driving 365 horses and mules headed to the Central Valley. Returning to the wild, Smith wrote of "feeling somewhat like that of a prisoner escaped from his dungeon and his chains." He could resume trapping and continue his search for the Buenaventura River.

The rain continued, and the valley became a maze of river channels. The men built rafts to ferry their supplies. They forced the animals to swim through swift currents. Two men deserted. Trapping as they went, they traveled up the valley along the present-day Sacramento River. Smith thought this wide river was the Buenaventura.

In the spring, the trappers reached the end of the valley. It was rimmed by mountains that "encircle the sources of the Buenaventura," Smith wrote. With disappointment, he concluded that the Buenaventura River was a myth in the minds of mountain men. His goal then became to reach the Columbia River. In April of 1828, Smith led his men toward the coast. "My route was in the direction of a Gap in the Mountains through which I intended to pass."

On to the Columbia

Through the gap in the mountains and beyond, Smith found a maze of canyons and forested ridges. "The traveling

California's Coast Redwood Trees

California's coast redwoods live to be more than two thousand years old. Many are taller than New York's Statue of Liberty.

extremely bad was made much more difficult and dangerous by the great number of horses which I had along," he wrote. Horses fell from cliffs and died in rivers below. Some days, the group traveled barely 1 mile (1.6 km). Nearing the coast, Smith saw his first redwood trees. He called them "the noblest trees I had ever seen." The redwoods, often shrouded in fog, made it impossible to find a route, so the men camped until the fog lifted.

Hungry and tired, the men reached the Pacific Ocean in early June. They were 300 miles (480 km) north of San Francisco. The Columbia River was 150 miles (240 km) away. Yurok Indians, who had never seen white men, traded shellfish for beads. Still, the men needed more food. Smith rode out to hunt to "alleviate the sufferings of my faithful party[,] and thanks to the great Benefactor[,] I found a small band of Elk." The men feasted, and Smith shared the meat with the Yurok.

From their coastal camp edged by forested hills, the men headed inland through brush and fallen trees. The next day, they returned to a long ocean beach. "I was in hope that we

Smith, with twenty men and more than three hundred horses and mules, struggled through thick forests on his way to the coast.

Traveling up the coast, the men and animals sometimes had to swim through the surf.

had passed all the mountains," wrote Smith. But a rugged coast lay ahead. The men and animals zigzagged from the beach, through mountains, and back to the beach. Indian tribes helped the men ferry their supplies and furs across coastal rivers.

Tragedy on the Umpqua

In July, Smith and his men reached the mouth of Oregon's Umpqua River. They had become the first white men to travel overland from California to present-day Oregon using a coastal route. When Indians of the Lower Umpqua tribe visited their camp, a tribal chief took an ax. Smith held the chief **hostage** until he stated where it was hidden. The chief and tribal members were offended by Smith's actions.

The next day, Smith and his men moved a few miles upriver. That evening, Harrison Rogers wrote in his journal that the Indians said the men were only a few days' travel from the Willamette Valley. Once in the valley, the men could easily reach the Hudson's Bay Company's Fort Vancouver on the Columbia River. Rogers dated his journal entry July 13, 1828. It was the last entry he would write.

Early the next morning, Smith, John Turner, and Richard Leland left in a canoe to look for a route to the Willamette Valley. While they were gone, one hundred Indians entered the camp and attacked the men to avenge the holding of the chief as a hostage. Fifteen men, including Rogers, were killed. Arthur Black escaped. As Smith and the men returned, Indians fired on them. Quickly, they paddled to the opposite shore where Smith climbed a hill. Seeing no life in the camp, Smith with the two men ran into the forest and found their way to the coast.

Fort Vancouver

Fort Vancouver was the headquarters of Hudson's Bay Company's Columbia District. Company trappers brought furs to the fort for shipment to Britain. They received food from the fort's orchards and fields, and their supplies were delivered by British ships.

Rescue and Reunion

Nearly three weeks later, Smith and the men with him limped into a village of Tillamook, who took them to Fort Vancouver. To their surprise, Arthur Black greeted them. He had arrived two days earlier. John McLoughlin welcomed the men. McLoughlin, a man with flowing white hair, stood

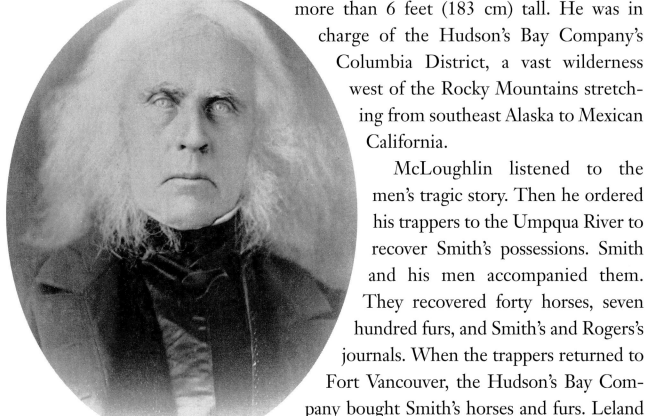

John McLoughlin of the Hudson's Bay Company welcomed Smith and his three men when they reached Fort Vancouver.

more than 6 feet (183 cm) tall. He was in charge of the Hudson's Bay Company's Columbia District, a vast wilderness west of the Rocky Mountains stretching from southeast Alaska to Mexican California.

McLoughlin listened to the men's tragic story. Then he ordered his trappers to the Umpqua River to recover Smith's possessions. Smith and his men accompanied them. They recovered forty horses, seven hundred furs, and Smith's and Rogers's journals. When the trappers returned to Fort Vancouver, the Hudson's Bay Company bought Smith's horses and furs. Leland and Turner had decided to stay at the fort, but Smith was anxious to rejoin his partners. Winter snows in the mountains, however, prevented his quick return.

While Smith waited for spring, he drew a map showing the routes he had followed. He shared his knowledge of the West with the Hudson's Bay Company men. Then one day, Smith received word that his partner, David Jackson, was trapping in the Rocky Mountains.

In mid-March, Smith, Black, and company trappers pushed canoes onto the Columbia River. After canoeing 450 miles (720 km) upriver, Smith and Black left the trappers and headed overland. They found Jackson in present-day western Montana. Their reunion was a mixture of sadness and rejoicing—sadness for those who did not return and rejoicing for those who did. They had not seen each other for almost two years. In August, the men were reunited with Sublette and his brigade in present-day eastern Idaho. After the fall hunt, the brigades went to the Wind River where they camped for the winter.

Smith, in a setting such as this, shared his stories with fellow trappers after they were reunited.

This photograph shows
a winter scene in the
Rocky Mountains.

Chapter Six

Trail's End

From a snowy camp, Smith wrote letters home on Christmas Eve of 1829. He had not been home for almost eight years. His letters expressed regret for his long neglect of family and church. To his father and mother he wrote, "Your unworthy son once more undertakes to address his Mutch [much] Slighted parents." To his oldest brother Ralph, he wrote, "Oh when shall I be under the care of a Christian Church?" He added that he would send money to help family and friends. "It is, that I may be able to help those who stand in need, that I face every danger."

A wagon train, led by William Sublette, brought supplies to the rendezvous of 1830. They were the first wagons to travel so far west.

Sublette carried Smith's letters to St. Louis and forwarded them to his family. From merchants, Sublette bought supplies for the next rendezvous and loaded them onto mule-drawn wagons. In July of 1830, Sublette arrived at the rendezvous point near the Wind River. His wagons were the first to travel that far west.

Smith's Last Rendezvous

It had been nearly four years since the firm of Smith, Jackson & Sublette was formed. During that time, it had become the dominant company in the U.S. fur trade. But trapping by the U.S. and the British companies had brought beaver to near extinction in many rivers and streams. Nevertheless, more companies were entering the fur trade. The three partners sold their business to a new firm, the Rocky Mountain Fur Company.

The partners loaded their wagons with furs and headed to St. Louis. On leaving the Rocky Mountains, Smith recalled that, "All the high points of the mountains then in view were white with snow; but the passes and valleys, and all the level country was green with grass." When the furs were sold, Smith's share of the profits made him rich.

Smith bought a home in St. Louis. Two of his brothers, Peter and Austin, came to live with him. He sent money to help his family and friends including, his mentor, Doctor Simons. He hired an acquaintance to copy his journals and to help produce a map of the West.

The Last Trail

Smith, however, was a mountain man, not a city dweller. He became interested in the Santa Fe trade. Settlers in the Mexican town were paying high prices for goods manufactured in the United States. His former partners, Jackson and Sublette, also became interested in the trade.

In April of 1831, the three set out along the 1,000-mile- (1,600-km-) long trail to Santa Fe. With them were seventy-four men, including Peter and Austin, and mule-drawn wagons loaded with goods. In May, the caravan crossed the Arkansas River in present-day Kansas.

The Mexican settlement of Santa Fe was Smith's destination when he left St. Louis in 1831.

Beyond the Arkansas River, they reached a broad, waterless plain. The mules began to weaken in the dry land. They were in the territory of the Comanche Indians, a tribe that fought to protect its lands against intruders. But as he had so many times before, Smith went ahead of his group to look for water. On May 27, 1831, near the Cimarron River, the Comanche killed Smith.

The Legacy of Jedediah Smith

Jedediah Smith spent just eight years in the American West. During that time, he had traveled more than 10,000 miles (16,000 km). In his short, adventurous career, he became one of the greatest explorers in U.S. history. His contributions to the knowledge of western geography were second only to those made by Lewis and Clark. They had explored a northern route to the Pacific Ocean. Smith was the first U.S. citizen to explore a southwest and central route.

Smith and his partners reported their discoveries to William Clark and the United States secretary of war. Their letters described the lands and the Indian tribes they had encountered. They provided vital information about the Mexican government in California and the British activities in the Pacific Northwest.

Information from Smith's journeys was used by explorer John Charles Frémont to guide his **expeditions**. Beginning in the 1840s, thousands of people followed Smith's route across South Pass on their way to settle the West. The wagon trail they used was pioneered by the wagons of Smith, Jackson & Sublette.

Today, highways and freeways wind along Smith's trails. Rivers bear his name. In northern California, redwoods grow in Jedediah Smith State Park. The ancient trees are a fitting tribute to this "young man of enterprise."

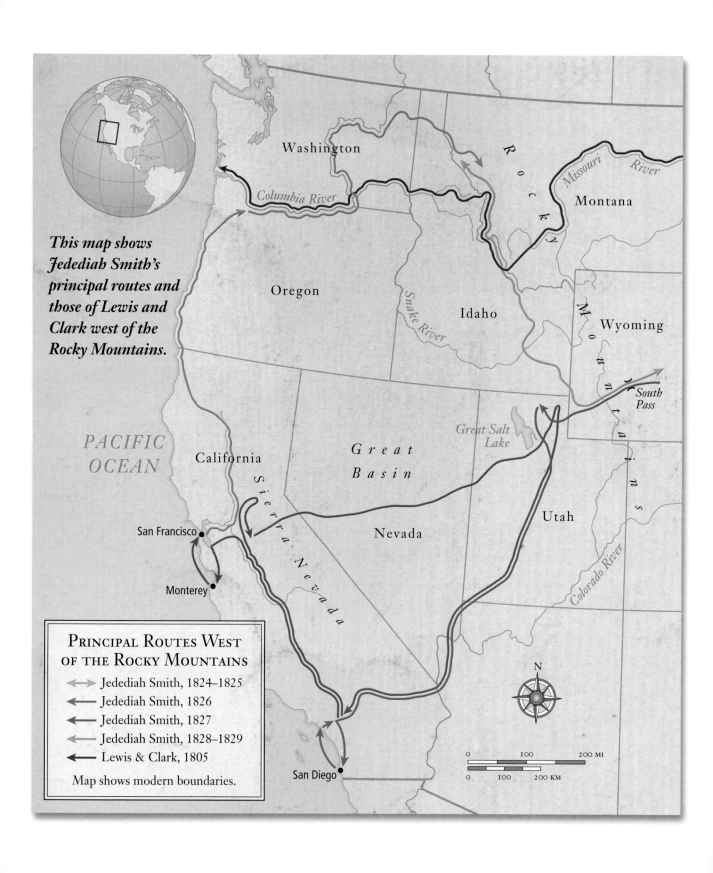

This map shows
Jedediah Smith's
principal routes and
those of Lewis and
Clark west of the
Rocky Mountains.

PACIFIC
OCEAN

Washington

Columbia River

Oregon

Snake River

Idaho

Montana

Missouri River

Wyoming

South Pass

Rocky

Mountains

Great Salt Lake

Great Basin

California

Sierra Nevada

Nevada

Utah

Colorado River

San Francisco

Monterey

San Diego

N

PRINCIPAL ROUTES WEST
OF THE ROCKY MOUNTAINS

← → Jedediah Smith, 1824–1825
← Jedediah Smith, 1826
← Jedediah Smith, 1827
← Jedediah Smith, 1828–1829
← Lewis & Clark, 1805

Map shows modern boundaries.

0   100   200 MI

0   100   200 KM

Timeline

1799	Jedediah Strong Smith is born in Jericho, New York, on January 6.
1811	The Smith family moves to Pennsylvania.
1817	The Smith family moves to Ohio.
1822	Smith arrives in St. Louis and is employed by the fur trading company of Major Henry and General Ashley. Smith heads west up the Missouri River on May 8.
1823	Smith fights in a battle with Arikara Indians.
1824	In March, Smith crosses South Pass and the Continental Divide.
1825	Ashley forms a partnership with Smith in the fur trading business.
1826	Smith and two friends start the fur trading company, Smith, Jackson & Sublette. In November, Smith becomes the first U.S. citizen to reach California by an overland route.
1827	Smith becomes the first white man to cross the Sierra Nevada and the first U.S. citizen to cross the Great Basin. In August, Mojave Indians assault Smith and his men on their return to California.
1828	Smith becomes the first white man to travel overland from California to Oregon using a coastal route. In July, Lower Umpqua Indians assault Smith's brigade. In August, Smith and three survivors arrive at Fort Vancouver.
1830	Smith, Jackson, and Sublette sell their fur trading business.
1831	Smith is killed by a band of Comanche Indians on May 27.

Glossary

brigade—a group of people organized to work together

buckskins—clothes made from deer hide

bullboat—a small, round boat made of elk or buffalo hide stretched over a stick frame

castoreum—a substance released from a beaver's castor glands that attracts other beaver

castor glands—a layer of cells that produce and release castoreum

confluence—the place where two or more rivers or streams join together

Continental Divide—the Rocky Mountain ridge that separates rivers flowing west from rivers flowing east

distillery—a place where liquor is made

evaporation—losing water into the air in the form of vapor.

expedition—a journey made for a definite purpose

game—wild animals hunted for sport or food

glass—a small telescope

Great Plains—the prairie region of the United States

hostage—a person who is held prisoner until certain conditions are met

keelboat—a large, shallow–bottomed boat used to carry freight on rivers

lacerated—with torn and ragged edges

mentor—a loyal friend and adviser

militia—a military group made up of people who are not professional soldiers

mission—the headquarters of a religious group

mountain men—men who roamed the mountains, where they lived and worked

pole—to move a boat forward by pushing on a pole

rendezvous—a prearranged place for a meeting

tepee—a cone-shaped tent made from animal skins

To Find
Out More

Books

Allen, John Logan. *Jedediah Smith and the Mountain Men of the American West*. New York: Chelsea House Publishers, 1991.

Burger, James P. *Mountain Men of the West*. New York: PowerKids Press, 2000.

Maynard, Charles W. *Jedediah Smith: Mountain Man of the American West*. New York: PowerKids Press, 2003.

Sundling, Charles W. *The Mountain Men of the Frontier*. Edina, Minnesota: Abdo & Daughters, 2000.

Videos

Challenge of the Trail. Skills of the Mountain Man, 1820-1840. Rocky Mountain College Productions.

Dress and Equipage of the Mountain Man, 1820-1840. Rocky Mountain College Productions.

Organizations and Online Sites

Jedediah Smith Society
University of the Pacific
3601 Pacific Avenue
Stockton, CA 95211
http://www.jedediahsmithsociety.org
The society collects and preserves information, artifacts, and documents about Jedediah Smith to be used for research. They publish a quarterly newsletter with articles about Jedediah Smith and related subjects. Each year, the society holds a rendezvous at a historic location.

Mountain Men and the Fur Trade
http://www.xmission.com/~drudy/amm.html
Explore this site to learn about the fur trade in the West. This site presents copies of trappers' journals, including a part of

Jedediah Smith's journal, mountain men images, and links to other sites.

Museum of the Mountain Men
Sublette County Historical Society
P.O. Box 909
Pinedale, WY 82941
http://www.pinedale.com/MMMuseum
Six rendezvous were held near present-day Pinedale. This online site includes an event schedule for Pinedale's annual Rendezvous Days, held the second week of July. It also presents information about the museum and other mountain men events.

White Oak Society
White Oak Learning Centre & White Oak Fur Post
Deer River, MN 56636
http://www.whiteoak.org/
This organization provides "living history" interpretations of the fur trade in the Great Lakes Region. There are links to Hudson's Bay Company archives, Native American languages, and living history societies. Read "The Beaver Fur Hat" and learn how this item of clothing was made.

A Note on Sources

After Jedediah Smith's death, his journals disappeared. His story was mostly ignored. Nearly one hundred years later, Maurice S. Sullivan obtained copies of part of Smith's journals from his descendants. Sullivan published them in 1934 in his book *Travels With Jedediah Smith*. Since then, more journals, documents, and letters regarding Smith have been found. These, with Harrison Rogers's journals, are included in Harrison C. Dale's *The Explorations of William H. Ashley and Jedediah Smith 1822-1829*, Dale L. Morgan's *Jedediah Smith and the Opening of the West*, and George R. Brook's *The Southwest Expedition of Jedediah Smith*.

While retracing more of Smith's trails, Sharlene and Ted did research at the Jedediah Smith Society's archives at the University of the Pacific in Stockton, California. Together, these resources made this book possible.

—*Sharlene and Ted Nelson*

Index

Numbers in *italics* indicate illustrations.

About the Authors

While growing up in California, Sharlene and Ted became familiar with the country where Jedediah Smith had traveled. They visited the missions where he stayed. They hiked along the rivers where he trapped beaver.

Both Sharlene and Ted attended the University of California at Berkeley and were married after graduation. Since then, they have pursued an interest in researching and writing about western history.

They have written books about West Coast lighthouses and the Columbia-Snake River Inland Waterway. Several of their books have been published by Scholastic Library Publishing, including *The Golden Gate Bridge* and *The Nez Perce*.

The Nelsons live near Seattle, Washington. When they aren't researching in archives or writing at their kitchen table, they are sailing, skiing, or hiking.